Short Vowels Phonics WORKBOOK

Danielle Johnson

©2023 Designed by Danielle

The contents of this book may not be distributed, resold, or reproduced in any form without explicit permission from the author.

© Designed by Danielle

Table of Contents

Short A

Write the word under the picture	3-5
Spell the word in the boxes	6-8
Color the short a words	9-10
Read and draw	11-12
Read, write, and draw	13
Writing sentences	14
Cloze sentences	15-18

Short E

Write the word under the picture	19-21
Spell the word in the boxes	22-24
Color the short e words	25-26
Read and draw	27-28
Read, write, and draw	29
Writing sentences	30
Cloze sentences	31-34

Short I

Write the word under the picture	35-37
Spell the word in the boxes	38-40
Color the short i words	41-42
Read and draw	43-44
Read, write, and draw	45
Writing sentences	46
Cloze sentences	47-50

Short O

Write the word under the picture	51-53
Spell the word in the boxes	54-56
Color the short o words	57-58
Read and draw	59-60
Read, write, and draw	61
Writing sentences	62
Cloze sentences	63-66

Short U

Write the word under the picture	67-69
Spell the word in the boxes	70-72
Color the short u words	73-74
Read and draw	75-76
Read, write, and draw	77
Writing sentences	78
Cloze sentences	79-82

Short Vowels

Write the word under the picture	83-85
Spell the word in the boxes	86-88
Color the short vowel words	89-90
Circle the words	91-93
Read and draw	94-95
Read, write, and draw	96-97
Writing sentences	98-99
Cloze sentences	100-104

© Designed by Danielle

Short A

Use the word bank to fill in the blanks.

Word Bank:

cat	grass	hat	map	bag
bat	flag	mad	fan	

_____

- - - - - - - - - - -

_____

_____

- - - - - - - - - - -

_____

_____

- - - - - - - - - - -

_____

_____

- - - - - - - - - - -

_____

_____

- - - - - - - - - - -

_____

_____

- - - - - - - - - - -

_____

_____

- - - - - - - - - - -

_____

_____

- - - - - - - - - - -

_____

_____

- - - - - - - - - - -

_____

© Designed by Danielle

Short A

Use the word bank to fill in the blanks.

Word Bank:

can	pad	clap	math	tag
van	crab	mask	sad	

© Designed by Danielle

Short A

Use the word bank to fill in the blanks.

Word Bank:

pan	mat	ran	wag	nap
man	glad	trap	sack	

_____
- - - - - - - - - - - -
_____

_____
- - - - - - - - - - - -
_____

_____
- - - - - - - - - - - -
_____

_____
- - - - - - - - - - - -
_____

_____
- - - - - - - - - - - -
_____

_____
- - - - - - - - - - - -
_____

_____
- - - - - - - - - - - -
_____

_____
- - - - - - - - - - - -
_____

_____
- - - - - - - - - - - -
_____

© Designed by Danielle

Short A

Spell each word in the boxes.

© Designed by Danielle

Short A

Spell each word in the boxes.

© Designed by Danielle

Short A

Spell each word in the boxes.

© Designed by Danielle

Short A

Color all the pictures that have a **short a** sound.

© Designed by Danielle

Short A

Color all the pictures that have a **short a** sound.

© Designed by Danielle

Short A

Read each word and draw it.

bag	rat	pat
can	fan	sad
cat	tag	man

© Designed by Danielle

Short A

Read each word and draw it.

mad	rag	flat
pat	bat	pan
wag	cab	sat

© Designed by Danielle

short a

Read the word. Trace the word. Write the word twice. Draw the word.

read/trace	write	draw
jam jam		
sad sad		
rat rat		
map map		
cat cat		

© Designed by Danielle

Short A

Write a sentence using the given word.

cat ....

_____

....

fan ....

_____

....

wag ....

_____

....

sad ....

_____

....

tag ....

_____

....

© Designed by Danielle

Short A

Use the word bank to fill in the blanks.

Word Bank:

had	sat	fan
lap	dad	pack

Sit in my _____.

We _____ so much fun!

My _____ is funny.

He will _____ his bag.

I am your biggest _____.

The cat _____ on the mat.

© Designed by Danielle

Short A

Use the word bank to fill in the blanks.

Word Bank:

mad	bat	bath
can	tap	van

She drove the _____.

I am _____ at you.

A _____ flew over us.

I _____ help you with that.

Did you _____ me?

I need to take a _____.

© Designed by Danielle

Short A

Circle the word that completes the sentence.

I put it all in my big _____.	bag wag
Did you _____ me?	tap lap
He put his _____ on his head.	mat hat
I do not want to be _____.	last mast
She likes to pet the _____.	pat cat
He looks _____ the box.	at mat
Do you want to play _____?	bag tag
How _____ can you run?	past fast

© Designed by Danielle

Short A

Circle the word that completes the sentence.

The _____ is very fat.	pat rat
He _____ down over there.	sat mat
Wipe it up with a _____.	bag rag
Tim needs to take a _____.	cap nap
That makes me very _____.	dad mad
Hit the ball with the _____.	sat bat
I love my mom and _____.	had dad
Let's look at the _____.	map tap

© Designed by Danielle

Short E

Use the word bank to fill in the blanks.

Word Bank:

hen	dress	bed	egg	web
ten	shell	pen	nest	

_____

_____

_____

_____

_____

_____

_____

_____

_____

© Designed by Danielle

Short E

Use the word bank to fill in the blanks.

Word Bank:

men	check	sent	seven	tent
left	bell	leg	sled	

© Designed by Danielle

Name:_____

Short E

Use the word bank to fill in the blanks.

Word Bank:

less	best	gem	jet	rest
net	wet	test	cent	

_____

_____

_____

_____

_____

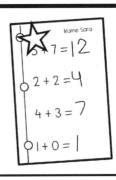

_____

_____

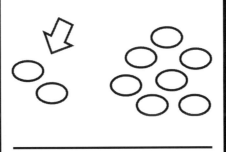

_____

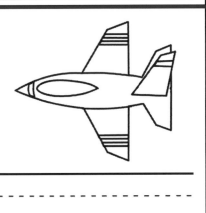

_____

© Designed by Danielle

Short E

Spell each word in the boxes.

© Designed by Danielle

Name:_____

Short E

Spell each word in the boxes.

© Designed by Danielle

Short E

Spell each word in the boxes.

© Designed by Danielle

Short E

Name: _____

Circle all the pictures that have a **short e** sound.

© Designed by Danielle

Short E

Circle all the pictures that have a **short e** sound.

© Designed by Danielle

Short E

Read each word and draw it.

wet	pet	beg
leg	bet	left
ten	net	pen

© Designed by Danielle

Short E

Read each word and draw it.

men	hen	bed
jet	red	met
test	belt	fed

© Designed by Danielle

short e

Read the word. Trace the word. Write the word twice. Draw the word.

read/trace	write	draw
pet pet		
yell yell		
neck neck		
check check		
ten ten		

© Designed by Danielle

Short E

Write a sentence using the given word.

red ⟩ ....
....

set ⟩ ....
....

beg ⟩ ....
....

let ⟩ ....
....

pen ⟩ ....
....

© Designed by Danielle

Short E

Use the word bank to fill in the blanks.

Word Bank:

dress	let	tell
peg	step	pen

Hang it on the _____ .

My new _____ is pretty.

My _____ is out of ink.

Don't _____ on the bug.

Can I _____ you a joke?

I will _____ you have it.

© Designed by Danielle

Short E

Use the word bank to fill in the blanks.

Word Bank:

met	red	best
ten	fell	shell

The boy _____ off his bike.

The walls are _____ .

This _____ was in the sand.

Have you _____ my mom?

There are _____ kids here.

She is the _____ player.

© Designed by Danielle

Short E

Circle the word that completes the sentence.

Do you want to _____ my dog?	pet met
You have very long _____.	legs reds
Will you _____ it on my bag.	set bet
You like to _____ for stuff.	wed beg
Will you _____ me come over?	let pet
My cat needs to go to the _____.	vet set
She will use a _____ to write.	men pen
Do you like pink or _____?	bed red

© Designed by Danielle

Short E

Circle the word that completes the sentence.

I will sleep in my _____.	red bed
Have you _____ your fish?	ted fed
Hang it up on the _____.	peg leg
Have you _____ my mom?	set met
I _____ you can win it!	bet let
She has a lot of _____.	pep bet
This rag is very _____.	wet set
The spider is in the _____.	web men

© Designed by Danielle

Short I

Use the word bank to fill in the blanks.

Word Bank:

bin	fish	gift	six	zip
ship	chick	pig	lip	

_____

_____

_____

_____

_____

_____

_____

_____

_____

35

© Designed by Danielle

Short I

Use the word bank to fill in the blanks.

Word Bank:

mix	kit	fin	mitt	hill
kid	sick	pin	bib	

_____

_____

_____

_____

_____

_____

First Aid

_____

_____

_____

© Designed by Danielle

Short I

Use the word bank to fill in the blanks.

Word Bank:

rim	hid	chin	in	win
milk	twin	hit	lid	

© Designed by Danielle

Short I

Spell each word in the boxes.

© Designed by Danielle

Short I

Spell each word in the boxes.

© Designed by Danielle

Short I

Spell each word in the boxes.

© Designed by Danielle

Short I

Circle all the pictures that have a **short i** sound.

© Designed by Danielle

Short I

Circle all the pictures that have a **short i** sound.

© Designed by Danielle

Short I

Read each word and draw it.

him	sit	twin
twig	**fix**	**hit**
kit	**fin**	**wig**

© Designed by Danielle

Short I

Read each word and draw it.

bib	hip	fish
pig	kid	pin
win	lip	six

© Designed by Danielle

short i

Read the word. Trace the word. Write the word twice. Draw the word.

read/trace	write	draw
kid kid		
six six		
gift gift		
hill hill		
pig pig		

© Designed by Danielle

Short I

Write a sentence using the given word.

fix ....

....

sit ....

....

kid ....

....

lip ....

....

tip ....

....

© Designed by Danielle

Short I

Use the word bank to fill in the blanks.

Word Bank:

sit	pick	fix
tip	win	if

It is hard to _____ just one.

My team will _____ .

I'll go _____ you go, too.

Will you _____ down?

Do not _____ the cup over.

He can _____ the car.

© Designed by Danielle

Short I

Use the word bank to fill in the blanks.

Word Bank:

mix	his	chips
dip	skip	big

I like to _____ in the yard.

That is a _____ house.

She ate some _____ .

He will _____ up the batter.

I'll take a _____ in the pool.

I like _____ red hat.

© Designed by Danielle

Short I

Circle the word that completes the sentence.

Will you help me _____ it?	fix sit
The boy fell into the _____.	kit pit
You need to make a _____.	list bit
It is not okay to _____.	fit hit
This dress does not _____.	mitt fit
There is a big _____ here.	kid hid
Put the _____ on top of it.	bid lid
Can I have a _____ of that?	lip sip

© Designed by Danielle

Short I

Circle the word that completes the sentence.

She will _____ it up.	mix pit
I see a shark _____ in the water.	tin fin
That is a very _____ dog.	wig big
The _____ is pink.	dig pig
Can you do a _____?	flip slip
The ball hit the _____.	win rim
Let's _____ a hole.	big dig
I hope we _____ this game.	win wig

© Designed by Danielle

Short O

Use the word bank to fill in the blanks.

Word Bank:

blocks	dot	frog	sock	pot
log	dog	box	lock	

_____

_____

_____

_____

_____

_____

_____

_____

_____

© Designed by Danielle

Short O

Use the word bank to fill in the blanks.

Word Bank:

hot	mom	moth	rod	drop
dog	jog	pop	doll	

_____

_____

_____

_____

_____

_____

_____

_____

_____

© Designed by Danielle

Short O

Use the word bank to fill in the blanks.

Word Bank:

hop	chop	stop	shop	rock
fox	mop	pot	odd	

_____

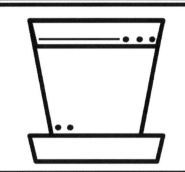

_____

_____

_____

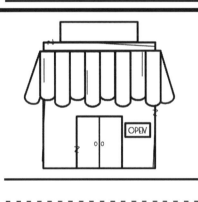

_____

_____

_____

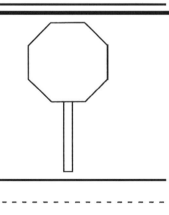

_____

© Designed by Danielle

Short O

Spell each word in the boxes.

© Designed by Danielle

Short O

Spell each word in the boxes.

© Designed by Danielle

Short O

Spell each word in the boxes.

© Designed by Danielle

Short O

Circle all the pictures that have a **short o** sound.

© Designed by Danielle

Short O

Circle all the pictures that have a **short o** sound.

© Designed by Danielle

Short O

Read each word and draw it.

hog	fox	mop
sob	stop	rot
fog	top	hot

© Designed by Danielle

Short O

Read each word and draw it.

hop	lock	dog
pot	box	sock
log	on	pop

© Designed by Danielle

short o

Read the word. Trace the word. Write the word twice. Draw the word.

read/trace	write	draw
sock sock		
box box		
shop shop		
dog dog		
block block		

61

© Designed by Danielle

Name:_____

Short O

Write a sentence using the given word.

not ⟩ ....
....

log ⟩ ....
....

hop ⟩ ....
....

dog ⟩ ....
....

stop ⟩ ....
....

© Designed by Danielle

Short O

Use the word bank to fill in the blanks.

Word Bank:

drop	lot	hot
dog	top	sock

Put the _____ on the jar.

My _____ has a bone.

That is a _____ of food.

It is too _____ in here.

Do not _____ your books.

The _____ has a hole in it.

© Designed by Danielle

Short O

Use the word bank to fill in the blanks.

Word Bank:

mop	off	boss
lock	shot	not

She _____ the ball.

I am _____ going there.

My _____ is very nice.

I need to _____ the door.

I will _____ the floors.

He fell _____ the bed.

© Designed by Danielle

Short O

Circle the word that completes the sentence.

The bunny likes to _____.	top hop
I have a _____ of friends.	not lot
Put it all in the _____.	box bop
Stack the _____ on top.	log lot
We need to sweep and _____.	top mop
She is _____ going with us.	pot not
Put the _____ back on.	mop top
This blanket is very _____.	loft soft

© Designed by Danielle

Short O

Circle the word that completes the sentence.

Tom _____ a new pet.	lot got
Turn the T.V. _____.	on not
It is too _____ in here.	got hot
The _____ is in his den.	box fox
My _____ wants to play.	dog log
I will sleep on the _____.	cot cob
The flower is in the _____.	not pot
He likes to eat corn on the _____.	lob cob

© Designed by Danielle

Short U

Use the word bank to fill in the blanks.

Word Bank:

nut	mug	bun	fun	cut
sun	dug	bug	drum	

© Designed by Danielle

Short U

Use the word bank to fill in the blanks.

Word Bank:

cub	pup	run	bus	bunny
duck	stump	tub	nun	

_____

_____

_____

_____

_____

_____

_____

_____

_____

_____

_____

_____

_____

_____

_____

_____

_____

_____

© Designed by Danielle

Short U

Use the word bank to fill in the blanks.

Word Bank:

jug	cup	shut	rug	up
gum	truck	mud	thumb	

© Designed by Danielle

Short U

Spell each word in the boxes.

© Designed by Danielle

Short U

Spell each word in the boxes.

© Designed by Danielle

Short U

Spell each word in the boxes.

© Designed by Danielle

Short U

Circle all the pictures that have a **short u** sound.

© Designed by Danielle

Short U

Circle all the pictures that have a **short u** sound.

© Designed by Danielle

Short U

Read each word and draw it.

bug	rub	bun
tub	luck	up
mug	hug	pug

© Designed by Danielle

Short U

Read each word and draw it.

fun	cup	hut
mud	tug	run
rug	duck	sun

© Designed by Danielle

short u

Read the word. Trace the word. Write the word twice. Draw the word.

read/trace	write	draw
rug rug		
sun sun		
bug bug		
up up		
duck duck		

© Designed by Danielle

Short U

Write a sentence using the given word.

hug > _____

_____

sun > _____

_____

run > _____

_____

rug > _____

_____

up > _____

_____

© Designed by Danielle

Short U

Use the word bank to fill in the blanks.

Word Bank:

cut	fun	hug
us	jump	run

Come with _____.

I _____ on the track.

I gave my dad a _____.

She will _____ it up.

That trip was _____.

He will _____ up and down.

© Designed by Danielle

Short U

Use the word bank to fill in the blanks.

Word Bank:

rug	up	duck
drums	dug	sun

Don't look at the _____.

The cat sat on the _____.

He likes to play the _____.

The dog _____ a hole.

A _____ swims in the pond.

Look _____ at the sky.

© Designed by Danielle

Short U

Circle the word that completes the sentence.

Can you _____ fast?	fun run
Do not look at the _____.	sun tug
Will you give me a big _____?	lug hug
This is a lot of _____.	bun fun
I will _____ it out.	cut rut
Will you _____ my back?	rub run
Do not hurt the little _____.	mug bug
Wipe your feet on the _____.	mug rug

© Designed by Danielle

Short U

Circle the word that completes the sentence.

I have tea in my _____.	hug mug
That is very high _____.	up cup
I am in the _____.	hut dug
That _____ is so soft.	pup up
Sam will _____ softly.	hum hut
We _____ a big hole.	rug dug
What is in your _____?	cup cut
My dog is a _____.	pug mug

© Designed by Danielle

Short Vowels

Use the word bank to fill in the blanks.

Word Bank:

pig	egg	fan	cup	mop
lip	pot	hen	cat	

_____

_____

_____

_____

_____

_____

_____

_____

_____

© Designed by Danielle

Short Vowels

Use the word bank to fill in the blanks.

Word Bank:

bag	fish	box	pen	ship
bat	cub	log	nest	

© Designed by Danielle

Name:_____

Short Vowels

Use the word bank to fill in the blanks.

Word Bank:

fin	map	web	mad	sun
bed	mug	pot	dog	

© Designed by Danielle

Short Vowels

Spell each word in the boxes.

© Designed by Danielle

Short Vowels

Spell each word in the boxes.

© Designed by Danielle

Short Vowels

Spell each word in the boxes.

© Designed by Danielle

Short Vowels

Color the pictures the correct color.

red = Short A	blue = Short E
green = Short I	purple = Short O
yellow = Short U	

© Designed by Danielle

Short Vowels

Color the pictures the correct color.

red = Short A		blue = Short E	
green = Short I		purple = Short O	
yellow = Short U			

© Designed by Danielle

Short Vowels

Circle the correct spelling of each word.

pup
pip

mitt
mutt

bag
bug

fox
fax

dot
dut

flug
flag

hit
hat

sick
sock

© Designed by Danielle

Short Vowels

Circle the correct spelling of each word.

frog / frag

cot / cat

tab / tub

desk / disk

cut / cat

fish / fosh

math / moth

pun / pen

© Designed by Danielle

Short Vowels

Circle the correct spelling of each word.

duck
dock

gum
gem

beg
bag

nun
nen

run
rin

lop
lip

ill
ull

not
nut

© Designed by Danielle

Short Vowels

Read each word and draw it.

bat	bed	mix
pop	tip	box
pet	bug	fan

© Designed by Danielle

Short Vowels

Read each word and draw it.

sun	hat	leg
web	top	pin
cab	rug	kid

© Designed by Danielle

short vowels

Read the word. Trace the word. Write the word twice. Draw the word.

read/trace	write	draw
bat bat		
egg egg		
pig pig		
cup cup		
dog dog		

© Designed by Danielle

short vowels

Read the word. Trace the word. Write the word twice. Draw the word.

read/trace	write	draw
hat hat		
red red		
sun sun		
log log		
twig twig		

© Designed by Danielle

Short Vowels

Write a sentence using the given word.

pet ....

....

bag ....

....

hug ....

....

hot ....

....

fit ....

....

© Designed by Danielle

Short Vowels

Write a sentence using the given word.

fox _____

_____

up _____

_____

tap _____

_____

fin _____

_____

red _____

_____

© Designed by Danielle

Short Vowels

Use the word bank to fill in the blanks.

Word Bank:

not	fix	bad
bed	kids	fun

The _____ are having fun.

He is _____ at the store.

Can you _____ my hair?

You will make your _____.

That was so much _____!

She had a _____ day.

© Designed by Danielle

Short Vowels

Use the word bank to fill in the blanks.

Word Bank:

hug	log	let
rag	had	pick

We _____ a good time.

I love to _____ my dog.

Let's _____ up the trash.

My mom _____ me stay up.

Use a _____ to wipe it up.

The kids sat on a _____.

© Designed by Danielle

Short Vowels

Circle the word that completes the sentence.

Put on your _____.	hat
	hut
Can you _____ it out?	cut
	cup
My dog can _____.	kit
	sit
The bunny can _____.	hop
	tip
Look at the _____.	bop
	map
He _____ a big hole.	rug
	dug
Can I sit in your _____?	lap
	cup
She _____ a good job.	did
	pig

© Designed by Danielle

Short Vowels

Circle the word that completes the sentence.

You need to chop the _____.	log sit
It will not _____ in the box.	hit fit
The frog is on the _____.	log bit
Can I _____ your dog?	kit pet
The egg is in the _____.	bet nest
Let's ride in the _____.	cat cab
The _____ is in the den.	cub big
Can I have a _____?	hug fin

© Designed by Danielle

Short Vowels

Circle the word that completes the sentence.

I have a new _____.	bag sit
The cat is in my _____.	lap log
The dog will _____ his tail.	wag bag
I _____ you are good at this.	bat bet
The _____ is in the cab.	man tan
Can you _____ my bike?	fat fix
Take a _____ of water.	sip hip
I will step on the _____.	big bug

© Designed by Danielle

Made in the USA
Las Vegas, NV
24 March 2025

20032831R00059